Scottish Witches *and* Wizards

H. M. Fleming

GOBLINSHEAD
Musselburgh

Scottish Witches *and* Wizards

First Published 2001
© Martin Coventry 2001

Published by GOBLINSHEAD
130B Inveresk Road
Musselburgh EH21 7AY Scotland
tel 0131 665 2894; *fax* 0131 653 6566
email goblinshead@sol.co.uk

British Library Cataloguing in Publication Data
A catalogue record for this book is available from the
British Library.

ISBN 1 899874 34 8

Typeset by GOBLINSHEAD using Desktop Publishing

Contents

Foreword

This book is about witches, wizards and witchcraft. It tells the stories about a number of people who were accused of witchcraft in Scotland between the sixteenth and eighteenth centuries. It does not intend to sensationalise the events or to make any comment about witchcraft, ancient or modern but merely to present the information in a clear and interesting manner.

All the people involved were real – not the work of fiction or imagination. Much of the information which has been used was found in official minutes from bodies such as the Privy Council, the Justiciary Court and church records. Other details were found in later histories or accounts published in the nineteenth century.

The book is divided into three sections: introduction, magic and cases. The first section – introduction – gives a background to different theories about witches and witchcraft. It explains what witches were accused of doing and how they were identified. It then explains how a witch was processed through the courts to execution. The second section – magic – looks at the practice of witchcraft. What they did and how they did it using spells, charms and potions. The final section is devoted to different cases some typical and some more unusual which occurred from the late sixteenth century up to 1724. Some of the cases involved ordinary people, and others individuals of higher social standing. All of the cases resulted in tragic deaths of both accused and often their victims, as in the case of Lady Foulis and the Erskine brother and sisters. There is also an index.

While doing some of the research for this book I have been struck by a feeling of sadness for all those involved, both accused and their alleged victims. People were frightened, live was tough and difficult, and an explanation for misfortune was needed. Witches were an acceptable explanation for the law, the church and the ordinary people. There were, however, times when the tone was lightened by snippets of information which, although not intentionally funny, illustrated the human concerns and fears of the population. Ellen Gray who was tried and found guilty for witchcraft in 1598, was accused of having bewitched Thomas Riddell, from Slains, so that 'his wand lay nevir doune'. He later died from this uncomfortable condition. Perhaps Gray had found an early version of Viagra!

In another case from East Lothian in

1644, Andrew Kerr was investigated for being a wizard and charmer of animals. The evidence for this accusation was that one of Kerr's cows had exploded in a rather dramatic fashion. The cow had died and swollen and Kerr was seen to make an incision in its belly. A burst of wind emitted from the carcass which was followed by blue and red flames. This whole episode had so frightened his neighbours that five of them appeared as witnesses. Kerr confessed that his mother had taught him how to use charms to treat animals which he had used successfully for several years. The church reprimanded Kerr and told him to appear in sackcloth before the North Berwick kirk session. As this was not deemed a case of witchcraft, unlike Gray, Kerr was not tried in a court of law and so escaped execution.

Although most of those who were accused of witchcraft were executed some managed to survive - blowing up a cow was certainly less threatening than causing the death of a man, no matter by what method.

The examples used in this book are only a small sample of witchcraft cases recorded in Scotland but hopefully they will give the reader an insight into the phenomenon.

HMF, Edinburgh, 2001

Scottish Witches *and* Wizards

Introduction:
Who and Why

W hat was witchcraft? Who were witches? What did they do? Why were they accused? Who accused them? What were their crimes? What happened to them?

So many questions and so many possible answers. Stories about witches and wizards seem to have always intrigued people – partly due to a bit of fear and awe – and today's current revival of interest in the subject is not so unusual.

With the Harry Potter books, J K Rowling has tapped into a topic which has challenged and stimulated society for many generations. In the past, people may have believed in the potential of the power of witches and were frightened of it. Contemporary official records include details about investigations, trials and executions of those accused. There are also some personal accounts by those who witnessed trials or were involved in them in some official capacity, such as lawyers, churchmen or witnesses to an execution.

Later accounts of witchcraft and witches, many from the nineteenth century, stressed how primitive our predecessors were, both to have believed in, and to have persecuted, certain individuals. Current attitudes are less critical and judgemental of past behaviours. In the increasingly material and scientific society of the twenty-first century, there is perhaps at most a need for, or at least a fascination in, this very non-scientific subject.

The connection between witchcraft and the supernatural has contributed to continued interest in the subject. We are often interested in things which are beyond our physical reality or understanding. Religion provided one system of belief and comprehension of how things worked for most societies. The rules and beliefs of the dominant religious organisation influenced what was perceived as being opposed to it and therefore regarded as witchcraft. In other words, the church and priests identified what was acceptable and what was not – the latter then often coincided with the practice of witchcraft. Those who claimed to have special knowledge and skills to heal or provide some comfort were a threat to the organised church, and so were regarded as their enemies.

Since witchcraft was seen as a crime against religion, the pursuers of witches and wizards were very likely to be theologians and priests, and the church as an organisation.

The religious interpretation is only one viewpoint. Another theory about why witches and wizards were regarded as criminal, or figures of fear, is more functional than religious. This approach was popular for a time, although it also has its restrictions. Witches and wizards were sometimes used as scapegoats and were blamed for others' misfortune. Therefore they could be justifiably punished. If people experienced a crop failure or the loss of animal stock, if their cows lost their milk or the milk did not churn, or if a member of a family took a serious and sudden illness, then the acceptable explanation was to blame another person or witch who would then be punished.

Those who accused, prosecuted and punished witches in this case were more likely to be ordinary members of society who could resort to both the church and the law to pursue their case. Witches were therefore a threat to, and the enemies of, society as a whole, not just particular groups.

Although these two interpretations are both valid, both need further qualification. Belief in the power of witchcraft existed in Scotland, as elsewhere, and it

offered a functional explanation about how
things worked or happened in nature. Witchcraft was also dualistic – it offered society
access to useful powers, as well as harmful
ones, at the same time. If black witchcraft was
the cause of illness or other problems then
white witches – or charmers – could be consulted for advice about how to treat illness or
remove the curse. One person's witch was
another person's charmer.

This paradox meant that people who were
identified as witches and wizards could at
worst be feared, or at best treated with a
degree of caution. They could provide
communities with healing advice, fortune
telling, love potions, finding lost or stolen
goods, and protective charms or counter-
magic. Yet witches and wizards were very
often themselves threatened by the rest of
society.

Scotland, along with the rest of Europe,
encouraged and supported by both the
church and the law, moved towards the
criminalising of all practitioners of witchcraft,
whether it was black or white.

By the late sixteenth century, and into the
seventeenth, it was the witches who had more
to fear from their neighbours and communities than the other way around.

Identifying a Witch

What made a witch a witch? Was simply being labelled or called one sufficient, or was knowledge about a specific set of practices or beliefs necessary?

In Scotland, the identifying and legal processing of a witch was quite a long and complicated business. The first stage involved accusations from witnesses, who were often neighbours or people who were known to the accused person. Sometimes this included other witches who would name their alleged accomplices in their confessions. In many cases, the confession was obtained by torture. The first people of authority who could be involved at this stage were from the church, either local ministers and elders, or even lay members, of the kirk session. Local council officials such as the baillie or provost, as well as local landowners, could also be involved.

If the allegations were regarded as sufficiently serious, then a commission of inquiry would be applied for – this usually resulted in a trial in a court of law.

The substance of complaints which were directed at the accused included many local and personal anxieties and concerns. The most frequently expressed worries were that witches and wizards had caused some harm or 'maleficium', such as the death of an animal, destruction of food or drink, or personal or family illness. These were often the primary features in an accusation.

A particular individual may also have gained a dubious reputation for practising witchcraft, or some form of magical art, over many years. This bad reputation, combined with the details of the particular harm, would only help to support the case against them.

There were, however, specific features that were used for the identification of witches in Scotland, as well as throughout Europe. The key components of accusation and evidence centred on the demonic pact and attendance at the witches' meeting or 'sabbat' – although these areas were of more interest to the church and the law than to ordinary folk.

These features were emphasised and described in detail in demonological tracts – such as *Malleus Maleficarum* or 'Hammer of Witches', and *Daemonologie,* the latter written by James VI of Scotland – which were written and published between the fifteenth and seventeenth centuries. These works gave both the church and the law the legal framework which they could use to identify witches categorically.

The demonic pact or the bond between the Devil and the witch was a rejection of both God and Christian ideology and doctrine. The sabbat or the witches' meeting, where many of the rituals and worship of the Devil took place, was seen as an inversion of the ritual of Christian worship and ceremony. The pact where the witch was the Devil's servant or inferior, was the rejection and inversion of Christian baptism and it was usually sealed with the taking of a new name or a nickname, and other specific actions. In their confessions, accused witches would describe how they held one foot with one hand and touched their head with the other while they swore allegiance to Satan.

Another important physical feature of the demonic relationship was evidence of the Devil's mark. This was a mole or some other insensitive skin tag on which, according to demonologist theories, the Devil, or the witch's familiars, would suck.

Devils and Demons

The descriptions of the Devil and other demonic spirits in the contemporary accounts are quite varied. Sometimes they fitted the stereotypical image of a horned and hoofed dark beast but, in other confessions, the Devil also appeared in human or animal form, or sometimes both.

On a few occasions, the demonic presence was seen and experienced as a combination of a meteorological manifestation and physical form. Some cases included references to whirlwinds which then took the shape of a man. Sometimes the Devil appeared as a dog or a cat, and then changed into a man. Quite often the man was young and good looking – rather than old and ugly – and his clothes came in a variety of colours, not just black as might have been expected. Blue bonnets, brown coats, green coats and bonnets, and grey clothes were just as common as black cloaks and hats.

The Devil – also known as Beelzebub, Auld Nick, Satan, Lord of the Flies, Lucifer or the Earl o' Hell – was not the only form of demonic power that early-modern society understood. Other demonic-type beings who were mentioned in the accounts included fairies and elves.

It has been suggested that fairies were simply a metaphor or an alternative identity for the Devil rather than a completely different form of demonic power.

For some, the fairy figure was a preferable, or more acceptable, image to use in place of the black figure of Satan, although they were one and the same. However, other theories suggest that fairies were quite distinct from the Devil. They were also spiritual or supernatural beings but, whereas the Devil was evil and harmful, fairies were neutral or at least morally ambiguous. They could use their powers for both good and bad, and witches who reported meeting fairies may have hoped that this relationship was more acceptable to their questioners than a contract, or a bond, with the Devil.

The ritual of the demonic pact also included sexual relations for female witches. The Devil promised to help these women and give them special powers, but in return for this they had to sleep with him. In some cases, the Devil also gave the witches what seemed at first to be coins or money, but by the next morning their new-found wealth had turned to stones or pebbles.

Although the promise of money – albeit usually a very small amount – might have been quite an acceptable temptation for some, for many Scottish witches it was not money which was on offer but, more prosaically, food and drink. The majority of ordinary folk were not wealthy, and survival during the sixteenth and seventeenth centuries was often a struggle. According to a good number of confessions, the Devil did not promise great riches or trappings of wealth, simply that his servants would not want for anything and they would have enough to eat and drink. It would be unfair to claim that those who turned to witchcraft were simply greedy or only tried to use their powers for themselves.

Their lives and motivations were more complicated than this.

The practice of the sabbat or witches' meeting may have been linked to this idea of enjoying food, alcohol and ceremony. Many of the descriptions and confessions include references to drinking, dancing, eating, music and singing – most of these activities were being actively discouraged by the church by the seventeenth century.

It was claimed that at these meetings witches and wizards – both men and women – would not just congregate to eat and drink,

12

but they would worship the Devil and participate in a variety of sacrificial and magical rituals. The coven of exactly thirteen – an inversion of the disciples of Jesus – is an artificial concept and the numbers involved in the groups were usually less or more than this. According to many of the confessions, however, these groups would meet at specific places, at a particular moor or clearing, and at certain special times, such as Halloween or Easter.

Some of the confessions mentioned the use of unbaptised children's corpses or animals in performing some particular harmful spell or charm. Malefice or harm was of more importance to those of the same social status as the accused than the details of the demonic pact. The loss of a source of food or income, or the sudden illness or death of a loved one, were all very significant and traumatic, and some system of compensation was important.

On the other hand, the church and the legal authorities were more concerned with the demonic features than just incidents of malefice. They put more stress on the pact, the sabbat, any association with other witches, the renunciation of baptism and the location of the Devil's mark.

Neighbours might accuse a suspected

individual first, perhaps informally, or an
accused witch might name a conspirator in
their confession, but it was the church and the
law who would then pursue the accusation
formally. Most witches would be accused
individually, but in some cases they could be
part of a larger group. Often accusations had a
ripple effect and one accusation would lead to
several more, each of which would, in turn,
lead to several more, so creating a panic or
witch hunt.

Processing an Accused Witch

In Scotland the first official witchcraft act was passed by parliament in 1563, although there had been some trials which included witchcraft in the accusation before this date.

According to many accounts the last witch executed was in Dornoch in 1727 and the act was modified in 1736, although not repealed completely.

Indeed, the last person from Scotland to be charged under the witchcraft act was Helen Duncan, a spiritualist and medium from Callander, who was accused of witchcraft during the Second World War.

It was claimed that during a seance she had communicated with a sailor who had been killed at sea. The War Office had not revealed any information about the sinking of that particular ship, because it feared it would harm morale, and the government were worried that Duncan was a spy. Duncan was found guilty and imprisoned.

Of course this case had very little in common with those from the sixteenth and seventeenth centuries, apart from fear of the witch or warlock, which was common to all.

During the one-hundred-and-seventy-three years between 1563 and 1736, it has been calculated that there were approximately three-thousand accusations – although fewer executions, of course – in Scotland. Although there were accusations throughout the two hundred years, there were also five periods during which time witchcraft accusation reached panic levels – or at least peaked. These were in 1590-2, 1597, 1629, 1649, 1660-2. Because these appear to coincide with other national political and religious events (such as the Covenanting times, the Civil War, and the Restoration of the Stewart monarchy) they have received most attention.

There were also, however, many cases of accusation and trial outwith these years, and it is clear that fear of witchcraft was an important and ever-present aspect of life in Scotland during these two centuries.

Not all cases of witchcraft followed the same route from accusation to trial, but there were some features which were common to many.

The first accusation was often made to a local kirk session and many cases would be dealt with at this level. The complaint would be investigated by the minister and elders, counter accusations might be made, and the evidence of the witnesses assessed.

If the case was not seen as being too serious, then those involved could disciplined within the local community at this stage. This punishment would usually take the form of public penance, and the guilty person would appear in sackcloth before the local congre-gation and pay a fine of money.

If the accused did not comply with the decision or satisfy the kirk session, the church could excommunicate those involved. The church was a powerful mechanism of social control in the seventeenth century, and the amount of exchange of information which went on between churches and ministers was remarkable for its time. Individuals who appeared in new parishes needed to produce evidence of their good character and behav-iour. If this documentation was not produced then they could be ordered back to their original location, or banished.

In other words, those who failed to com-ply with the orders of the kirk might find it difficult to find safe hiding elsewhere.

If it was felt the case was more serious, then further evidence would be collected from witnesses. The accused would be questioned by the minister and elders in an attempt to get a confession. The accused could be held in the local tolbooth if there was one or, in smaller villages, often in the kirk itself although permission for 'watching and warding' needed to be obtained from the central authorities prior to imprisonment.

Accusations of malefice or a bad reputation were not themselves sufficient proof of guilt. The confession of the demonic pact was the single most important piece of evidence.

Confessions about the specific rituals of witchcraft and sorcery, and association with other witches, were useful extras but were not crucial to the overall case.

To extract the required confession, torture would often be used. Sleep deprivation, crushing of the feet and ankles using the boots, thumbscrews or 'pinniwinks', removal of nails and insertion of needles into the nail beds, and the rack were all forms of torture that were used throughout the country.

Another aspect of the torture process or ordeal was the use of the rather disreputable profession of witch pricker. These were individuals who publicised their ability to identify witches scientifically by locating the Devil's marks. They would travel the kingdom touting for business and were regularly employed in certain places. He, although some of them were women, would insert needles into suspicious marks or moles to find out whether the accused could feel pain at the spot. It was believed that these marks were insensitive to pain and would not bleed.

By the mid-seventeenth century, the authorities began to question the honesty of these individuals and some were themselves imprisoned for being charlatans.

After this initial stage of investigation, it was necessary to get a commission to try the accused. This meant a group of six or so named men were given permission to gather evidence on a more formal basis. A commission could be granted by the king, the Privy Council, the Parliament or, after 1649, the Committee of Estates. A court trial was held by the Central Court of Justiciary in Edinburgh or Circuit Courts which covered the rest of the kingdom.

If the commission of inquiry was granted, then the local ruling elites would become involved officially. In many cases, however, they were probably already involved in the investigation on an informal basis before this stage. The commission would include local landowners, ministers and other men who had some social standing or position. The elders of a kirk session were often council baillies, clerks or provost and some of them could also be appointed to a commission. The local sheriff was also often a member of the commission.

At the official trial witnesses, who might be related to the alleged victim and who were likely to have a personal grudge, were permitted to appear. Other witnesses who could only repeat circumstantial evidence or hearsay were also allowed.

Lawyers for some of the accused tried to argue that these witnesses did not provide adequate proof of the guilt of their clients. They maintained that some of the things which had happened were likely to be entirely natural, rather than being caused by any supernatural power.

In other words, some lawyers began to question the whole idea of supernatural or magical powers. Most juries, however, convicted on the evidence of the confession rather than the accounts of malefice, despite the often convoluted legal arguments concerning the reality of the supernatural by both the prosecution and defence.

Sometimes the accused refused to confess or later tried to deny previous confessions, but this had little effect. Once a guilty verdict was reached, the accused was sentenced to death. Most Scottish witches were strangled, or 'wirreit', before they were burnt, although some were burnt alive.

Although there were many trials in Scotland not all of those who were accused stood trial. One method of trying to get an acquittal or abandonment of a trial, which was used by some defence lawyers, was to suggest that the accused was simple, demented or mentally incompetent and so was unable to stand trial.

A few trials were delayed due to pregnancy but were not abandoned completely. Some of the accused were acquitted on the grounds of maturity. In most cases, however, old age or infirmity was no excuse and many of the accused were quite old when they stood trial. Children were usually regarded as too young to stand trial. Others died in prison before their trial or sentence, sometimes by their own hand, and there were others who escaped and fled as far and fast as they were able.

The cost of investigating and trying a witch was not cheap but accusations were not made on economic grounds or in the hope of gaining financially from any execution. Local communities did not benefit from the sharing out of the accused's property, which in most cases was minimal anyway. Indeed, communities usually had to fund the cost of the whole process themselves. The accused had to be held in prison and fed, and watched by members of the community which cost money. The pricker charged a consultation fee, the court officials cost money, and the lawyers on both sides received payment for their services.

Even the cost of the final execution had to be met by the pursuers, including the services of the hangman and the fuel for the burning.

Magic: *Spells, Charms and Potions*

M any witches were tried and executed in Scotland – around two thousand to three thousand – mostly between 1563 and 1736. There were others, however, who were accused but who were not tried in a court of law. There were also those who claimed to practise charming or white witchcraft, rather than black witchcraft or magic. These individuals would give advice about the treatment of illness, lost property, affairs of the heart and other common concerns. Although they were sometimes investigated by the church or other authorities, they did not suffer the same fate as those found guilty of demonic pact, witchcraft and sorcery.

T he features of the crime of witchcraft have been outlined, but the actual practice of witches and wizards is also interesting. What did both the accusers, and those who confessed, describe in order to demonstrate that magic or witchcraft had been used? What spells, charms, rituals, potions, curses were utilised in order to either harm or heal? Did they use spoken verses or incantations, stick pins in wax figures, administer potions made from strange herbs, plants and animal parts, tie knots in threads or animal hair, use fire or poison, walk over rivers or bridges or to other boundary markers, use baked bread or eggs, sprinkle water from wells or springs over the afflicted person or animal, or use some special object which was claimed to have special power? And how did the power work?

The recorded accounts from witchcraft investigations and trials describe the use of all of these objects and rituals.

Witches and wizards, and the rest of society during the sixteenth and seventeenth centuries, believed that harm was caused by transference and that it could be removed by the same process. The harm was transferred to a person or animal through the use of intermediate objects such as potions, an item of clothing, or the use of images or models which represented the intended victim. The victim might also be harmed by a group of witches carrying out a specific ritual at a particular place or time. It could also be caused in an indirect fashion by the use of a spoken curse or simply by the power of the 'evil eye' or *droch suil*.

James VI wrote in *Daemonologie* that people would use many methods to protect themselves from the power of the evil eye. This included weaving rowan twigs into the hair of their animals to protect and cure them.

Other divination rituals involved using sieves and shears to identify culprits and thieves.

Society believed that witches and wizards were extremely powerful. According to *Malleus Maleficarum,* a witch could manifest herself as an incubus or succubus (male or female demons which would sleep with the person and cause nightmare terrors or visions); influence men's minds to love or hate; prevent pregnancy; cause impotence; change shape; cause the possession of the mind and body of others; kill children and babies; injure cattle; and cause hailstorms, tempests and lightening.

They could steal the milk of cows by sitting down in their own house with their milk pail and stick a knife or some instrument into the wall. The witch would then appear to be 'milking' the knife or stick with her hands. The witch would then acquire the milk from a cow in the neighbourhood which was lactating. The milk would flow from the stick or knife.

To make it rain, the witch would dip a piece of wood in water and sprinkle the water in the air.

Witches would make a wax images in order to bewitch people or cause them an injury by piercing it in some way.

Some of the rituals or meetings of witches may have taken place on specific days or time of year. The most powerful times of the year would appear to be have been the quarter days of Beltane and Samhain, which were Celtic calendar festivals.

The celebration of Beltane or 1st May was associated with the coming of spring, fertility and growing crops, and marked a change in the agricultural year.

Samhain or Hallowmass – 1st November – was the first day of winter. It marked the end of the agricultural year and preparation for winter.

Both festivals involved the use of fires and a number of protective rituals. As they were associated with change and with gathering spirits, they were also seen as periods of vulnerability. Divination games and rituals were carried out during these festivities.

In some cases, the accused witches described meeting the Devil and their fellow witches at Beltane or Samhain. The North Berwick witches were reported to have held their second big meeting on All Hallows Eve

– the night before Samhain – in 1590. Andrew Man from Aberdeen attended ceremonies at All Hallows Eve in the sixteenth century. Isobel Gowdie confessed to meeting with other witches in the form of rooks at Lammas time, another quarter festival on the 1st August.

Indeed, many of the rituals and features of the sabbats described by the accused witches – which included drinking, singing, eating and the use of fires – corresponded quite closely with the celebration of important pre-Christian calendar festivals. This does not mean, however, that witchcraft was an alternative religion or pre-Christian system of belief which continued to be practised by a section of society into the eighteenth century. What is more likely is that ordinary people continued to observe older customs which may have been purely symbolic but which made people feel lucky or hopeful. Much of Scottish society was rural and entirely dependant on agriculture, and had no access to modern medical practices or techniques, for either man or beast.

One method of casting a charm involved shape changing which, although quite unusual, was recorded in a certain number of cases.

The witch would appear as, or change herself, into another form – usually an animal and particularly cats. She would often be accompanied by the Devil, either in human or animal form.

A typical case is that of Isobel Greirson who, it was claimed, had entered the house of Adam Clark, a neighbour, as a cat and, along with several other cats, had made a 'great and fearful noise and trouble'.

Another tale of a shape-shifting witch is illustrated by an incident associated with a member of the Kerr family of Littledean, in the Borders, in the seventeenth century. This laird was much disliked for his violent actions against his religious enemies. One day he was out riding and came upon a pretty young woman who broke a thread in two, laughing at him.

This symbolic action was regarded as a form of cursing. Littledean fled the scene but later became obsessed with finding the beautiful girl again. He attempted to capture her by returning the site of their encounter but the only thing that he saw was a hare. On his return home the laird told his friends that he had been chased by first one hare, then another and a third, until there was a whole group of them. He had attempted to slash at

them with his sword and finally managed to
severe the paw of one of the hares.

He then managed to outrun the hares and
reach the safety of his home, but when he
took out the hare's paw to show his friends it
had turned into a women's hand indicating
that the girl or witch had transformed herself
into a hare.

The idea that a witch could still be injured
while in her animal form was recorded in a
number of cases and is not unique to
Scotland.

Animals, particularly cats, featured in a
number of rituals – either as a familiar, as
the Devil or the witch herself in another
physical form. Beigis Todd described how she
took a new cat to the iron gate of Seton in
East Lothian where she passed it nine times
through the gate. She then took the cat to a
sabbat where the Devil named the cat
Margaret.

The witches at North Berwick used a
number of animals, including dogs and toads.
In 1722 Janet Loch, who it is claimed was the
last witch executed in Scotland, was accused
of turning her daughter into a pony so that
she could ride on her to the sabbat meeting.
It was also claimed that the Devil had shod
the girl while she was in the form of a pony

and that this had caused the lameness of her daughter's feet and hands.

Night-flying was closely associated with shape-shifting. In Europe, night-flying was usually aided by the application of a magical potion, and it has been suggested that the sensation of flying may have been caused by the hypnotic or narcotic effects of different herbs and fungi. Although some continental cases described the ingredients which were used to make the potion – including dead children – there are few specific details in the Scottish material.

There are occasional references to witches being taken up and transported by a whirlwind. Janet Cock from Dalkeith in Midlothian was reported to have summoned the Devil in the form of a wind which transported Christian Wilson to Niddrie Marischal just outside Edinburgh. Those cases, however, which included some mention of the accused appearing elsewhere at night, either as themselves or in the form of an animal, clearly indicate the belief in night-flying. The use of brooms on which the witches travelled or rode through the sky would appear, however, to be a modern invention, although it is hinted at in the case of Isobel Gowdie.

Some witches were so powerful they did not need to use any spells or objects and could simply affect their victims with a look from the evil eye. This was often referred to as being forespoken. Witches could touch or strike directly but another, less direct method, was to use words or curses.

In Scotland, verbal curses were often called malisons. The power of the tongue was indeed often mightier than the sword, at least when accusations were made against those suspected of witchcraft. The actual words of the curses were not recorded in the testimony, but it can be presumed they must have been quite fearsome.

The case of Agnes Finnie from Edinburgh, however, who was accused of sorcery and witchcraft in 1644, has an unusual number of verbal curses. She was accused of cursing Janet Grinton who later took a serious illness and was unable to eat. Grinton died after fourteen days. It was claimed that Agnes had cursed Janet saying: 'Go your way home, you shall not eat more again in this world' after an argument over the poor quality of herring which Agnes had sold.

Agnes also cursed John Buchanan saying 'John, go away, for as you have begun with witches, so shall you end with witches'. He later took a fearful illness which lasted for seven weeks.

When she called Euphamie Kincaid a drunkard, Euphamie then retorted by saying 'If I am a drunkard, you are a witch'. Finnie replied: 'If I am a witch, either you or yours shall have better cause to call me so'. Within two days Euphamie's daughter had broken her leg.

In another altercation, Finnie shouted at Christian Dickson, who owed her some money, 'The devil ride about the town with you and all yours'. Margaret Williamson was cursed with the following 'The devil blow you blind' and she later lost the sight of her left eye.

The power of Finnie was extended to her daughter who was accused by Mausie Gourlay of being a witch's child. Finnie's daughter Margaret, who had obviously inherited her mother's sharp tongue, replied: 'If I be a witch's child, the devil take your soul afore I come again'. The victim of the curse was not Mausie, but her husband, who later became frantic and stark mad 'his eyes standing out in his head in a most fearful and terrible Maner'. Agnes Finnie was obviously not someone who bit her tongue when she was angered – but she was the one who suffered the most in the end.

Most witches would use specific items to enchant people, animals or goods using the process of transference. Isobel Gowdie of Auldearn described how she used the corpse of an unbaptised child in a ritual. She would take finger and nail clippings, grains of meal and bunches of kale (a type of cabbage) which were all finely chopped together and mixed with the child's corpse. This mixture was then put under dung heaps on a neighbour's land. The result of this ritual, or spell, was that the neighbour lost his crop, and Isobel and her fellow witches benefited from the meal which they then used to feed their own families.

Witches were also accused of meeting at kirkyards, where they took a number of dead bodies from their graves and dismembered them in order to use parts in their spells and incantations.

Some witches confessed to, or were accused of, causing impotence, although this seems to have been quite rare in Scotland. This could be accomplished by the tying of knots in a handkerchief or cloth. This method of curtailing other people's actions by knots was also believed to delay childbirth.

This motif is seen in a number of ballads and folk tales, and indeed the loosening of knots or tangles in hair, sheets and other household items was regarded as an important ritual of childbirth. In the ballad *Willie's Lady*, the hero Willie had married a woman who was not of his mother's choosing. When the time arrived for the wife to give birth, progress was unexpectedly delayed. The wife told her husband to go to his 'mother again, that vile rank witch of vilest kind'. The mother responded determinably: 'Of her young bairn she'll ne'er be lighter, Nor in her bower to shine the brighter. But she shall die and turn to clay, and you shall marry another may'.

As luck would have it, however, the young couple had the services of a brownie (a domestic spirit that would do chores and help around the house) who gave them some wise advice. 'Ye doe go to the market place, and there ye buy a loaf of wax. Ye shape it bairn and bairnly like, and in twa glassen een ye pit'.

The couple were then advised to invite the mother-in-law to the christening of the new 'baby'. When she arrived they were to watch her reaction and listen carefully. The mother was heard to exclaim: 'Oh wha has loosed the nine witch knots that was amo that ladie's locks? And who has taen out the kaims of care that hangs amo that ladie's hair?' At this the brownie was immediately able to loosen the knots, and remove the combs in order that the childbirth could progress normally and the mother-in-law was exposed as a witch.

This 'spell' did not only use knots and combs, but a bush of woodbine, a young goat, and a tight left shoe.

Jane Craig, another accused witch, was said to have caused the death of a child using three stones. Jane had been excluded from the birth of her sister-in-law's child. As a result of this social slight, Jane had rubbed and smoothed the child with three enchanted stones, which she had obtained from her own mother. The child later died, and the incident was used as evidence against Jane at her trial.

Illness could be transferred by a variety of objects. An accused witch was said to have laid an illness on a boy by placing a black card under the door of his father's house. Isobel Greirson, mentioned earlier, was also accused of laying an illness on a man, William Burnett, by throwing a piece of raw meat at his door.

Wax figures or images made of clay or butter were another means by which witches could harm their intended victims. Wax figures and a picture of James VI were used by the North Berwick witches, and Lady Foulis had figures of her victims made from butter. Isobel Gowdie made a figure of clay which she hoped would destroy the Laird of

Park's male children. The figure included arms, legs, feet, hands, eyes, mouth and nose and was laid on a fire until it was red hot. It was hoped that by this method all the living sons of the laird, and those not yet born, would perish.

As well as being burnt, the figures were sometimes stuck with pins or stabbed with some other implement. Again this was in order to cause the victim injury, pain or trouble in a particular part of their anatomy.

Other objects that were believed to cause harm were often called 'elfshot' or fairy darts. These prehistoric flint arrow heads were regarded with suspicion, mixed with wonder, by sixteenth and seventeenth-century society. They did not appear to be man-made and therefore the explanation that they must have been created by the fairies was accepted, although witches might also use them. It was said that they were shot at animals and, if they pierced the skin, the animal would take ill.

Like other aspects of fairy lore, however, the magic of elfshot was ambiguous as it could also be used as an antidote to any potential harm. If pieces were found on the ground, or perhaps unearthed during ploughing, they could be used as an amulet or protective charm against witchcraft when worn round the neck of the beast or person.

Sometimes the enchantment or spell would be in the form of food or drink which would be forced on their victims. Many accounts describe how these gifts of food were rejected for fear that they would bring harm. Ironically, the victim usually seemed to fall ill even though the food or drink had been refused.

An example of a potion administered to the Archbishop of St Andrews is found in the poem *The Legend of the Bishop of St Androis*. He sent for a witch to help him with his many illnesses and her recommendations included herbs, stones, books and bells, men's members and south-running wells, palm-crosses and knots of straw, the paring of a priest's toenails, St John's Nut and a four leaf clover, Holy water, amber beads and another forty or so 'weeds'.

Another service 'witches' or charmers offered was help in finding lost goods or predicting the future.

The former usually involved identifying the thief using a combination of rituals. A local charmer, John Turnbull, was asked to find a thief and it was recorded that he wrote the name of four women on a piece of paper.

Being able to write was still relatively unusual in the seventeenth century, and this ability alone makes John Turnbull unusual. The paper was cut into pieces which were then put into water. Turnbull then took a nail and asked the women to hold it in their hands. The women did so in turn, but it stuck to the hand of one of them. As further proof of her guilt the piece of paper with her name on it was wet but those with the names of the others were dry, even though they had all been in the water.

The ability to predict the future did not always benefit the teller. It seems strange that if they were able to foretell events then why they did not at least attempt to avoid their own misfortune?

The case of Kittie Rankie, a French girl and accused witch, who worked at Abergeldie Castle during the late sixteenth century illustrates this. She was also known as Catherine Frankie or Kitty Rankine and was maid to the laird's wife, Margaret. According to the local legend, Margaret's husband was delayed returning home to his wife, and Margaret ordered Kitty to use her skill to find out why he was late. Kitty used water and a wooden bowl, and informed her mistress that her husband was otherwise employed on board a ship by the attractions of his mistress. Margaret ordered Kitty to summon a storm, which she duly did and the ship was reportedly sunk at sea, drowning all on board.

Instead of showing any gratitude, the mistress then threw Kitty into the dungeon and she was later tried for witchcraft. It was claimed that she was burnt, and later that strange noises which coming from the dungeon and other manifestations were caused by the ghost of the young French woman. There is no written record of Kitty's trial, however, and so the story may not be accurate.

The famous Brahan Seer, Kenneth Mackenzie, shared a similar fate around 1670. He was asked by the wife of his patron, Isabella, Countess of Seaforth, what was delaying her husband in Paris. Kenneth told her that he was involved with a French woman. Isabella was so angry that she had Kenneth burned in a barrel of tar on Chanonry Point in the Black Isle.

Before he died, however, Kenneth went on to predict the many woes, early deaths and misfortunes that were to strike the family.

Case 1:
Alison Pearson, Byrehill, Fife, 1588

During the sixteenth century, the Devil began to appear as an important feature in some witch trials. Not all accusations of witchcraft, however, included reference to being the Devil's servant, especially those cases which had some sort of political agenda or motive. Although many witch accusations and trials followed quite similar patterns, there were also a number of cases which were unusual or unique – which make them more notable.

The case of Alison Pearson is interesting because it had a number of unusual features. It featured the figure of the Devil, which was not unusual, but in Alison's case it was claimed he was her uncle, Mr William Sympsoun.

Alison was from Byrehill in Fife, and she was tried for sorcery and witchcraft in 1588. Aside from her association with the Devil, some of the interesting details in this case concern Alison's descriptions of fairies, the 'Court of Elfane' and her association with the fairies.

When she was twelve years old, her uncle William Sympsoun – a scholar and doctor of medicine – healed her of an episode of illness. After his treatment, however, she was left with a residual weakness, or loss of power, in her hand and foot.

William Sympsoun seems to have been a mysterious figure not so much because of his training in medicine - which in the sixteenth century was relatively unusual – but how and where he had acquired his knowledge. It was reported that Sympsoun had been taken from his father, the king's smith, when he was six years old, by an Egyptian. Egyptians were believed to be an exotic and mysterious race at this time, and were themselves the subject of an act of parliament forbidding their free movement about the country. This Egyptian was also said to have been a giant and he took the child back to the exotic east for twelve years where Sympsoun learnt the art and skill of medicine.

The implication was, of course, that he had learnt the Black Arts or sorcery, which were akin to witchcraft. According to Alison, it was Sympsoun who introduced her to the fairies. He was able to tell when the fairies would appear from 'middle earth' because he could hear the sound of a whirl wind which proceeded their arrival. Although Sympsoun was only six years older than Alison, she was reportedly extremely frightened of his power and authority.

Alison's account also described her experiences at the court of Elfane, where she claimed she spent seven years. At the fairy court there was much fun and merriment, including music from pipes, dancing and singing, and drink and food. Although much of the time that she spent with the fairies was good, it was also sometimes very bad. On occasions she would remember being taken away by the fairies to St Andrews or as far away as Lothian, but other times she would simply awaken in her own bed and not know where she had been.

According to Alison, she had no power over events herself as it was the fairies who controlled her movements. They also promised her rewards. One time a man in green appeared to Alison and promised her that 'if she would be faithful he would do her good'. The fairies could also be angry and, when she tried to talk about things to the authorities or other people, she claimed she was punished by losing the power of her left side.

Not all of Alison's experiences were negative, and as a result of her experiences with the fairies Alison claimed to have acquired the ability to heal disease using the fairies' methods. When she was at the fairy court, she saw them make special potions and lotions. The fairies would gather herbs before sunrise, then boil and distil them over fires to create magical salves and medicines.

She also confessed, however, that it was Sympsoun, rather than the fairies themselves, who had taught her about different diseases and which herbs and treatments to use to cure them. To support his claim, Sympsoun had told Alison about Patrick Adamson, the archbishop of St Andrews, who had reportedly consulted a witch about a number of his ailments. The archbishop suffered from fever, heart problems and general weakness. He was given a salve – or lotion – to rub in his throat, chest, stomach and sides.

Although it was not formally recorded, it is believed that Alison was executed in the usual fashion by being strangled and burnt at the stake.

Case 2:
Lady Katherine Foulis, Foulis, 1590s

Throughout Scottish history many murders or attempted murders were carried out for financial or political gain. These murders often involved more than one person and the plots could be quite convoluted. Death from injuries sustained during armed conflict, starvation while imprisoned, poisoned food, death by fire – these were all methods by which murder could be accomplished. It was sometimes claimed, however, that, along with the more prosaic methods of weaponry and poison, the murderers had also used witchcraft and sorcery to carry out the desired crime.

These accusations of witchcraft for political gain were unusual for a number of reasons. Many of these cases involved people of relatively high social and economic status, whereas most people who were accused of witchcraft were not wealthy people. The motive for this sort of crime was straightforward personal gain.

Many witchcraft accusations certainly involved malefice – or harm – which sometimes resulted in the death of a person or animal, but they did not usually result in financial or political advantage. Jealousy and revenge are strong emotions. They were often recognised as important factors in cases were a particular dispute resulted in a curse or frank exchange of insults – which could be used as circumstantial evidence in a trial.

In cases which involved the murder of an individual of high social status, there would appear to have been a good deal of cold-blooded premeditated plotting. The Devil had little to do with these cases: greed and ambition were powerful enough motivation.

On such case involved Katherine Ross who was the second wife of Robert Munro, the 15th Baron of Foulis. Robert Munro had two sons – Robert and Hector – and three daughters by his first wife. With Katherine, he had a further three sons and four daughters.

Lady Katherine, along with her younger stepson Hector, was accused of witchcraft, sorcery, incantation and poisoning. They appeared to have had a plan to murder Robert, the elder son who had inherited the

Barony of Foulis from his father, and Katherine's sister-in-law, Marjory Campbell, who was married to Katherine's brother, George Ross. The motives were purely financial – Hector would inherit his brother's title and George Ross would marry Robert's widow and gain her family money.

The accusations against Lady Katherine were both numerous and specific. They included the use of elf shot or arrow heads to injure or harm particular individuals, the use of a particular charm to bewitch, and the administration of rat poison. A number of servants were involved in the conspiracy and either procured the necessary items or poison, or administered or delivered the packages or food on their mistress's behalf. Some of the accusations against Lady Katherine included features of witchcraft, such as the use of elf shot and the bewitching charm. Others, such as the use of rat poison, were clearly far less about supernatural powers and more about straightforward murder.

According to the accusations, Katherine and her servants used butter to make images of Marjory and Robert: the two intended victims. Elf shot, or arrows, were then thrown at the images in order to damage them. Both of these were important elements of witchcraft belief and practice. The use of images to represent the intended victims was not unusual, nor was the use of elf shot. Although the use of butter was less common, the belief that wax or clay figures stuck with pins or roasted in the fire, so that the victims would be similarly afflicted, was widespread. Elfshot or arrows were believed to be used by fairies to injure humans and animals.

It would seem Lady Katherine was determined to achieve her objective and she did not rely only on supernatural powers to kill her victims. Taking a more practical approach, she also tried to poison them, on more than one occasion – although most of these attempted poisonings failed.

The accusations relating to the use of poison also involved a number of other people, both as accomplices and victims, including an unfortunate nurse who tasted the poison intended for her master and subsequently died.

One attempt involved the poisoning of a whole meal, which a number of the extended family ate, including Hector, her erstwhile accomplice, and his children. Fortunately for those involved, most of the poison appeared to have been spilt and so the attempt failed.

It was also claimed that Lady Balnagown, Katherine's sister-in-law, ate meat which had been poisoned. The poison was mixed with the kidneys of a deer which had been killed by a hunting party.

Although this case was from the late sixteenth century, there was no mention of demonic witchcraft or pact which became a feature of many later cases. Lady Katherine was accused of witchcraft – using elf shot and image magic, sorcery, having and using some knowledge of poison and other dangerous concoctions, and poisoning itself – but there was no reference to any association with the Devil. Perhaps Lady Katherine did not need the assistance of the Devil as she was dangerous enough using her own devices.

Katherine and Hector were tried, as were the servants who had also been involved in the various attempts. Many of them were found guilty but the main protagonists, Katherine and Hector, were found innocent of all accusations. This was perhaps not that surprising given the social status of the accused, giving them some distinct advantages over the servants when it came to the trial proceedings.

In Lady Katherine's case, the prosecutor

was none other than her stepson Hector, who himself was later tried. Secondly, Lady Katherine's carefully selected jury was also unusual. It was composed of men who were her social inferiors or who had some connection to the family, and so could be manipulated. Juries usually comprised men who were either socially equal or superior to the accused. Lady Katherine's jury delivered a not guilty verdict, which meant she escaped any punishment, as did her stepson.

High social status was not always enough to save a lady or lord. Lady Janet Douglas, widow of 6th Lord Glamis and sister of the Earl of Angus, was accused of witchcraft by James V, an accusation which also involved an attempt to poison the king. James V's motives appear to have been malice towards her family, extending to her, and she was almost certainly innocent.

The poor woman could not escape the king's hatred, and she was burned on Castle Hill in Edinburgh in 1537. Her ghost is said to haunt Glamis Castle.

Case 3:
North Berwick Trials, 1590

One of the most notorious witch trials in Scotland was held at North Berwick in East Lothian. It involved many people, both as accused and potential victims, from James VI right down to maidservants. The accused included people from the lowest social level, middling peasants, wives of landowners to Edinburgh burgesses or ruling class elites, and finally a Scottish noble.

The whole extended case turned out to be very complex – in part because it involved so many people and also because it has been the subject of many written accounts – but, like many other incidents, its origins were initially not very dramatic or serious.

The baillie depute in Tranent, another East Lothian town, one David Seaton, was suspicious about the behaviour of his maid Geillis Duncan. It transpired that Geillis was not spending every night in her own bed, and he wanted to know what she had been up to. Although it may seem a little odd that a master should be concerned about something as insignificant as the sleeping arrangements of one of his servants, at this time masters were responsible for all aspects of the behaviour of their entire household, including family members and servants.

At the same time, Seaton was, like many others, also aware of the threat of witchcraft and was anxious to root it out. As a further complication, Geillis, and one of the other accused, were reputed to be local wise women – healers or charmers – who advised people about illness. This familiarity with things supernatural only increased the likelihood of Geillis being a witch, since the two were so closely associated, at least to men like Seaton.

Seaton accused Geillis of witchcraft and had her arrested. Before getting any official permission, he started to torture Geillis – an acceptable method of extracting confessions in the sixteenth century – although initially she refused to confess. He used the pilliwinks on her, which crushed her fingers. Eventually he had her searched for the Devil's mark by a local pricker. When a mark was found on her neck, poor Geillis finally started to confess and in great detail.

She said she had had a pact with the Devil and had attended meetings with other

51

witches. She then accused others: Agnes
Sampson from Haddington, Bessie Thomson
from Edinburgh, Dr John Fian from Prestonpans, Janet Stratton, Donald Robson, Ritchie
Grahame, and Euphame MacCalzean and
Barbara Napier, both from Edinburgh. The
last two were also both related to Lord
Cliftonhall: Euphame was his daughter-in-law
and Barbara his sister-in-law.

Geillis was imprisoned and questioned
from December 1590 until June 1591. She
was finally executed with Bessie Thomson in
December 1591, a year after her first confession about the witches' meeting at North
Berwick. Just before her death, however, she
announced that everything she had said
previously about the others had all been lies –
which by then could do little or nothing to
save her or the others.

John Fian was one of the first of the rest of
the group to be arrested, questioned and
tried. He was imprisoned in December 1590
and executed only two months later in
January 1591. Fian seems to have been a
enigmatic figure and some of the information
about him only increased the mystery and
confusion. He had a number of aliases and
was referred to as John Cunningham, John
Sibbet, John Fean, and Dr Fian. He was the

schoolmaster at Prestonpans, but it was also recorded that he taught at Tranent. It was also claimed that he confessed to committing adultery with thirty-two women – he must have been a busy man.

Much of the information about Fian and the others comes from a published account of Fian and the others called '*News from Scotland*' which appeared during, or just after, the North Berwick witch trials. It is an anonymous pamphlet and, although it is claimed that it is a true account of the events, it is clear that it is an edited, and very likely an exaggerated, version of events.

The author of the pamphlet may have been involved in the trials in an official capacity or he may simply have attended them on a private basis. Since there is no way to authenticate the authority or veracity of the author, some of the detail contained in this publication may be fiction.

The account of Fian's exploits includes an episode which certainly sounds too fantastic to be true, and if it was true then it went very wrong. It was claimed that Fian had attempted to use love magic in order to attract a particular young woman. He asked her brother, one of his pupils, to bring him three of her hairs. The boy was unable to get the hairs and told his mother about the request. The woman then substituted hairs from one of her cows which were given to Fian. Fian then carried out the magical ritual using the cow's hairs. Within a short time, it was claimed, much to Fian's embarrassment, the cow began to follow him around rather than the girl.

Fian's confession gave many details about his relationship with the Devil. He was an educated and literate man, and his confession reflects this. Fian described how he had been dreaming about revenge when the Devil had appeared and promised him prosperity and riches in return for service.

His account of the North Berwick meeting described much more clearly an inverted religious ceremony than Geillis's version. Fian described the use of candles, sermons, prayers and preaching. He also described how new members were initiated into the group, how they worshipped the Devil, and how dismembered corpses were used as part of their rituals. Fian also told how the group had killed men, caused storms, ruined crops and destroyed livestock.

Since he was an educated man and able to write it was claimed that Fian was the Devil's clerk. Because of the very specific detail, and because he was educated, Fian's account might be seen to be more believable than some of the others who were uneducated and possibly credulous. Nevertheless, like the others, Fian was also tortured excessively – a rope was tied around his head and tightened, his legs and feet were repeatedly crushed in the boots. Any confession or account given under these circumstances was bound to be unreliable, and so Fian's version may have been no more accurate then any of the others.

Unusually Fian managed to escape from jail, after he appeared to have repented his crimes, but was recaptured quickly. He was again tortured, this time his fingernails were pulled out and nails driven into the tips of his fingers. Like Geillis, before his execution Fian denied that his confession was true, and he claimed – not unfairly – that it had been tortured out of him. In particular, he denied having any knowledge of the plot to drown queen Anne. However, like Geillis, he was strangled and burnt at the stake.

It was the connection to royalty that made James VI interested in this case. One of the claims made by Geillis Duncan was that the witches had plotted to kill him and his wife. Coincidentally, about six witches from Denmark had been executed for allegedly trying to cause storms in 1589 to prevent Anne from reaching Scotland, and news about this event arrived in Scotland in mid 1590.

From the end of 1590 James himself examined and questioned the suspects. Agnes Sampson was taken to Holyrood to be interviewed by the king, but she refused to confess. Agnes had earlier been subject to an investigation about accusations of witchcraft by the Haddington synod in 1589.

Like Geillis, Agnes eventually confessed after she had been tortured and searched, and she went on to name other people who had been involved: Katharine Gray, David Steel and Janet Campbell. She also named Barbara Napier and Euphame MacCalzean.

Sampson told the king that she had used magical charms, had attended coven meetings or sabbats, and had been involved in a plot to murder the king.

In her confession, she described how on All Hallow's Eve or Hallowe'en (31 October), two hundred witches had put out to sea in sieves. They carried flagons of wine with them and sailed to North Berwick. At the Auld Kirk in North Berwick, they had all participated in a session of dance and song which was presided over by the Devil. She claimed that Geillis Duncan played tunes on the Jews

Harp, a small musical instrument held between the teeth and plucked with a finger.

Sampson reported that the Devil made all the witches kiss his bottom, and that he had 'baptised' a cat which he then threw into the water. This was done in order to cause a ship wreck. The intended victims of the ship wreck were to have been the king and his new wife, Anne of Denmark.

James had been in Denmark for his wedding and it has been claimed that about this time he had become familiar with some of the elite ideas about demonic witchcraft which were circulating on the continent. James was also intrigued by a number of coincidences in Sampson's account.

On the journey to Denmark, his ship had experienced an episode of rough weather (not that unusual in the North Sea!). This ship survived but another of the fleet – a vessel carrying the queen's jewels and other presents – did sink on its way back to Scotland. It was also recorded that Sampson whispered in the king's ear the exact words which he and his wife had exchanged on their wedding night.

Agnes Sampson's confession became increasingly elaborate and incredible. She described how wax figures and animals had been used in their spells, and how spirits were invoked. One spell involved collecting the venom of a toad, which had been intended to be used to harm the king. The plan had been that an item of the king's clothing or property was to be obtained which would be used along with the venom. One of the king's servants, John Kers, had been asked to acquire the necessary item but he refused to help.

Agnes Sampson continued to 'confess' until January 1591, at which point she was found guilty and executed. Like the unfortunate Geillis, Agnes had been known as a healer and charmer who had knowledge of herbs and magical remedies.

Another of the accused, Barbara Napier, was a well-connected Edinburgh woman who was married to one Archibald Douglas. Unlike the others, she was able to afford defence council.

The main accusation against Napier was not that she was a witch, but that she had consulted witches – notably Agnes Sampson and Ritchie Grahame.

She had consulted Richard or Ritchie Grahame for some advice and treatment for vomiting for another woman Jean Lyon. Jean, who was pregnant, had asked Barbara to help her. Barbara was acquitted initially on the grounds that she herself was not a witch and had not personally carried out any sorcery or witchcraft. She was also found not guilty of attending the North Berwick meeting.

King James, however, was not happy with this verdict. He addressed the jury about the case and on points of law. With the king sitting in attendance at the court, the jury then changed their verdict and found her guilty. Napier's execution was delayed because she was pregnant, but the sentence was eventually carried out in 1591.

Richard Grahame was also questioned and later executed.

Like Barbara Napier, Euphame MacCalzean was also a well-connected Edinburgh woman. She was the daughter of Thomas MacCalzean, an advocate, and her husband was Patrick Moscrop, the son of another advocate. One of the accusations against Euphame was that she had used poison and witchcraft in an attempt to murder her first husband – an attempt which seems to have been unsuccessful. The impression of having been a rebellious, unloving wife only added to the likelihood that she was a witch.

The evidence that Euphame had used witchcraft on her husband had an alternative objective. It was also claimed that she had

consulted Agnes Somerville from Dunfer-
mline for advice about how she could get her
husband to love her rather than in an attempt
to get him killed. Euphame gave the woman
two of her husband's vests, which were to be
enchanted by being passed over water.

Unfortunately for Euphame, the charm did
not have the desired outcome so she then
tried to poison him and consulted other
witches who enchanted his doublet. After he
took ill, Patrick seems to have fled the country
in order to avoid any further danger to his life.

Some of the other accusations against
Euphame seem to have been about
personal disputes between the accused and
other people.

They included attempts at poisoning,
preventing marriages, the recovery of jewels,
and accusations of attempted enchantment
using clay or wax figures.

Euphame was also accused of having
attended a number of witches' meetings,
including the one at North Berwick, and that
she had made a wax image of James VI which
was used in an attempt to kill the king. She
was also involved in conspiring to sink the
king's ship. Along with Agnes Sampson,
Robert Grierson and the others, she was
accused of attempting to drown queen Anne

by throwing an enchanted cat in the sea at
Leith.

Euphame was found not guilty of attempting to kill her husband and some of the
other accusations but, despite having a
defence advocate, she was found guilty of
consulting witches, and using witchcraft and
sorcery. The plot to kill the king meant that,
like the others, her crimes included treason.
Unlike the others, Euphame was sentenced to
be burnt alive rather than being strangled first.
She was executed in June 1591.

The North Berwick trials were by no
means finished and the web of involvement continued to spread. By 1591, in part
because of the king's encouragement, Francis
Stewart, the 5th earl of Bothwell, was then
implicated in the crime of treasonable witchcraft.

Ritchie Grahame had told his inquisitors
that Bothwell had been behind the plots to
cause the death of the king. Bothwell had also
been accused by Geillis Duncan, and especially
by Agnes Sampson: part of a plot against him?

Bothwell was James's cousin and was the
nephew of James Hepburn, the 4th earl of
Bothwell, who had been Mary queen of
Scots's third husband. Although King James
and Bothwell had been close, they had later

become bitter rivals, and James took advantage of Bothwell's implication in the North Berwick witch trials to assert his royal authority over his former friend.

Agnes Sampson was reported to have claimed that Bothwell promised them gold, silver and food; and Janet Stratton declared that Bothwell had instructed them to attempt the murder of the king.

Not surprisingly, Bothwell denied the accusations but, although accusations of witchcraft for political means were relatively unusual in Scotland, he was imprisoned. In June 1591 a proclamation was issued which stated that Bothwell had used necromancy and witchcraft, had been the Devil's servant, and had attempted to murder the king. Like Fian, Bothwell managed to escape with the help of some powerful allies, but he was officially declared an outlaw – which made it difficult or even impossible for him to remain in the country as a free man.

The Bothwell situation continued for some years; in 1592 he was forfeited, which meant that all his property was taken by the state. Although officially declared a rebel, Bothwell remained at large and continued to be a threat to both James's person and his authority. Not surprisingly, Bothwell wanted to clear his name and reclaim his property, so in 1593 he led a successful coup against James and managed to take control of the government.

With the king in his power, Bothwell demanded a trial by his peers on the charge of witchcraft. Bothwell got his day in court and he was acquitted in August 1593.

The matter did not end there. After his acquittal, Bothwell's aggressive manner convinced others that he was a threat and, by 1595, James again managed to send Bothwell into exile – this time permanently.

Bothwell died in Naples in 1612 having lived for a time in France and Spain. He did not manage to distance himself from the 1591 witch hunt, and his reputation for necromancy followed him until his death.

James VI produced his own written account of witchcraft entitled *Daemonologie*. It was published after the trials, either in 1591 or 1597, and was claimed to be a rebuttal to the more moderate works about witchcraft written by Reginald Scot and Johan Weyer.

These two authors questioned the reality of witchcraft and argued that some of the so-called witches were often in more need of help than prosecution, as they suffered from melancholy. These works had been produced for some years but their influence was not very widespread, therefore the motive behind the publication of *Daemonologie* is more likely to have been because of James's personal experience and observations during the trials.

Many of the details and descriptions in the book are lifted from the accounts or confessions of those accused. James also attempted an analysis and discussion of magic, witchcraft, and the nature and power of supernatural spirits. His account presents the sabbat or witches' meeting as an inversion of a Christian religious ceremony: the Devil represented as preaching to his acolytes and presenting his naked bottom from the pulpit. *Daemonologie* appeared in London in 1603, the year James succeeded Elizabeth to the throne of England, and in 1604 the last English witchcraft act was passed.

James was himself not the impetus behind the 1590 witch trials. Instead, that pressure clearly came from local men who had a certain amount of influence and power. These included David Seaton and David Carmichael the minister at Haddington. Nevertheless, James's involvement gave these trials a significance which echoed down into the following century and beyond.

Case 4:
Andrew Man,
Aberdeen, 1598

At the same time as the North Berwick trials there was a another episode in Aberdeenshire which also started in 1590. After an initial outbreak there was a lull until 1596-7. Amongst those suspected was Andrew Man, who was accused of witchcraft and sorcery and of having been the Devil's servant for over 60 years.

Man's account of his experiences, which he gave in his confessions, included some interesting details, in particular those about his involvement with fairies. Fairies – also known as the 'good neighbours' – featured in Scottish witch trials in two main ways: they could grant special powers and knowledge, often related to healing, to chosen individuals; and they could be responsible for certain misfortunes, in the form of mischief and illness.

This dual nature of fairies was by no means unique to Scotland.

Andrew Man's relationship with the Queen of the Elves or Elphan started when he was just a young boy. Sixty years before, about 1538, the Devil, in the guise of a woman, came to his mother to help in delivering her child.

This image of the Devil as a female figure was quite unusual. The Devil was usually male, particularly when he had dealings with women.

Andrew was asked to bring some water to help the birth. In return he claimed that the Queen of Elves promised that he would have the power and knowledge to help and cure sickness.

Andrew also confessed that when he was older he had a physical relationship with the Queen of the Elves, and they had had several children together.

Man claimed that he could heal many illness, both of humans and animals. He described one healing ritual which involved blessing the afflicted person or animal, striking them on the face while holding a bird in his hand and saying: 'If you will live, live, and if you die, die', along with some other verses.

Man further confessed to curing the animals belonging to several local people, including the Laird of Kinnaird.

He also confessed that he had cured lady Kinnaird of the 'falling sickness' – a popular term then for what we know as epilepsy.

Man described a protective ritual which he carried out with the assistance of a spirit body called 'hind knight'. They measured wards, or enclosed pieces of land, and left four stones in the four corners of each ward. It was claimed that this ritual would provide protection for all the goods – animals or crops – within the boundaries, particularly from lungasüte (a disease of the lungs).

In his confession there are a number of interesting details about how sixteenth-century society perceived illness.

Illnesses were believed to be caused by some form of enchantment or bewitchment, which had been cast either accidentally or deliberately. The accepted antidote to this was to transfer the disease onto something or someone else – usually an animal rather than another person. Many of Man's treatments confirm this belief. He advised another man, Alexander Symsoun, to pass forward through a piece of unwoven yarn or wool. The next stage involved passing a cat backwards through the same piece of wool nine times. As this was carried out, Man recited blessings or prayers over the man and the cat. Later, when the man recovered, the cat took ill and died.

Man also used the skill and knowledge given to him by the Queen of Elves to steal cow's milk and corn from other people. To steal corn, or to ensure his crop would flourish, Man would strip the corn head from the straw and throw it into the rest of the crop saying, nine times: 'The dirt to thee and the crop to me'.

In his account, Man described the appearance and powers of the Queen of Elves, the Devil, and elves and fairies in general. The Queen could appear as young or old as she chose, and she would ride on a white coach. The Devil was known by a number of different names, and could take on a number of different appearances. He was sometimes known as Christonday, and could take the shape of a stag, a crow, or appear as a white angel.

The rest of the company of elves mostly looked like men and wore the same kind of clothing. Although they appeared shadow-like, they were much stronger than ordinary mortals. During their meetings or congregations the elves would sing and dance freely, and generally appeared to have had a great and merry time. Unusually, Man reported that there were several dead men in the company – either as fairies or more straight-forwardly as ghosts – including James IV (who died in 1513) and Thomas the Rhymer. The celebrations would take place in what seemed to be elegantly-decorated rooms with many lights and candles, food and wine. When he woke after these festivities, however, Man would find himself lying on the moor with no sign of the fine furnishings.

An unusual feature of Man's confession was his description of the Day of Judgement. According to Man, this would occur when fire would burn in the water. He explained that the year after this 'end of days' event would be extremely bad, but for those who survived there would be fourteen good years after this.

Man was found guilty of witchcraft and sorcery, and it is presumed that he was executed.

Case 5:
Robert, Helen, Isobel and Annas Erskine, Dun, 1613-14

In another trial for witchcraft which had a political motive, Robert Erskine and his three sisters, the grandchildren of John Erskine of Dun – one of the leaders of the Reformation church in the 1560s – were accused of the murder of their nephews, John and Alexander Erskine, in 1610.

Robert Erskine was charged with witch-craft, sorcery, consultation with witches, and poisoning.

On his deathbed Robert's brother, David Erskine, had stated that his two sons were to be tutored and supervised by another relative – John Erskine, minister at St Ceres – instead of their uncle. This meant that Robert was deprived of the financial benefits which were associated with tutoring two young men and being in charge of their estate. The lands and fortune of the Erskine of Dun family would legally pass to the two boys, not Robert.

In revenge or simply for greed, Robert plotted the demise of the children with his sisters. Firstly, two of the aunts proposed to David Blewhouse that he might help them in their scheme in return for 500 silver marks and some land. David Blewhouse refused.

The two sisters, Annas and Helen, then went to Janet Irving, who was known locally as a witch. Janet gave them herbs which she claimed would achieve the desired effect. Robert did not believe his sisters and went to see Janet himself. Janet assured him they would be successful, and the herbs were then soaked in ale.

The poisoned drink was given to the young boys, and very soon after they began vomiting. John Erskine, the elder boy, developed a dreadful disease – his skin turned black and he pined away in great pain and distress until his death. It was claimed that before he died he exclaimed: 'Woe is me, that ever I had right of succession to any lands or living! For if I had been born some poor cottar's son, I had not been so treated, nor wicked practices had been plotted against me for my Lands!' Alexander, the younger boy, although badly poisoned, appears to have survived for longer than his brother but also eventually died.

Robert Erskine confessed to his part in the plot to murder his nephews by poison. After his trial, he was executed by beheading at the Mercat Cross in Edinburgh in 1613.

The following year Helen, Isobel and Annas were tried for the same crimes. They were also found guilty and were ordered to be executed. The following year, 1615, Helen's life was spared by Charles I. She had been held in prison in Edinburgh for a year and it was felt that her involvement in the crime had not been as great as her sisters and brother. She was banished from the country for the rest of her life, on pain of death if she ever returned.

This was another case where political and financial gain were the objectives of a murder plot. To give the case further impact the accusation extended to include witchcraft and sorcery, but it was really one of straight-forward murder. There is no indication in the confessions or trial evidence that the Erskines made a pact with the Devil or other spirits. They had consulted with Janet Irving, a local woman, who may have had a reputation as a witch because of her knowledge of herbs – both beneficial and harmful – but there was no use of other forms of magic or super-natural powers such as incantation, invocation or bewitching. This type of accusation of using witchcraft for personal financial or political gain was relevant only to those who had access to property or power – and was still very unusual.

Case 6:
Margaret Wallace, Glasgow, 1622

Witches were often perceived as old, poor and unmarried, either widows or spinsters. Although many did fit this pattern, there were also others who did not. Witches could be male, young, occasionally middle-aged. They could also part of what was, during the seventeenth century, the middling class: those who had some social and economic status but were not nobility or even gentry.

Margaret Wallace was an example of this middling sort. She was the wife of John Dunning, who was a merchant burgess in Glasgow during the first part of the seventeenth century, and her trial for witchcraft, sorcery, charming, incantation, soothsaying and abusing of her fellow citizens gives us an insight into both the social history and the psychology of the time.

Margaret would appear to have been involved in a number of disputes or disagreements with other people in the neighbourhood, all of which may have contributed to the accusations levelled against her. Although there was some mention of demonic pact and attendance at sabbats or meetings, the most important accusations were those of laying-on and taking-off illness and consulting with another reputed witch.

Some of the details illustrate nicely the back-biting and petty disputes which existed in burgh communities. Margaret was also quite unusual in that she was able, because of the relative wealth and status of her husband, to afford a defence counsel, which included the advocates Alexander Peebles, Robert Lermonth and Thomas Nicolson the Younger.

Margaret's accusers included other Glasgow craft and merchant burgesses, with whom either Margaret, or her husband John, had had some form of argument or falling-out – and then, by extension, their relatives or neighbours.

One of the pursuers, Alexander Boig, was a smith who had fallen out with Margaret and her husband over payment for an anvil. Margaret had complained to Boig's landlord or master, but had received no recompense for the debt. It was claimed that she then cursed Boig.

Some of the other witnesses were rather

vague about specific events and their evidence was somewhat circumstantial. Other key witnesses for the prosecution were related to the alleged victims – and so might not have been entirely independent eye witnesses!

The first charge was that after a dispute with Cuthbert Creg, a cooper and burgess, she had uttered a curse which had caused him to suffer a sudden and debilitating illness. After some time, Margaret visited Cuthbert, at his request, during which time she felt his wrist, laid her hand on his chest, and mouthed some words. The next time she took him by the arm and told him to rise and walk, and he was now able to do.

There were a number of other charges which concerned the laying-on and taking-off illness, in some cases resulting in the death of victims.

One of the charges claimed that Margaret had cursed Robert Mure and had said: 'You shall go home to thy house, and shall bleed at thy nose a quart of blood, but shall not die until you send for me and ask my forgiveness'. Shortly after Mure died of a sudden illness.

Another accusation was that Margaret had taken ill when she was at Alexander Vallange's house. She sent for one Christiane Grahame –

a recently convicted witch – who, it was claimed, cured her using 'devilish charms'.

It was then claimed that the two women had returned to Vallange's house where they met Vallange's daughter at the bottom of the turnpike stair. Margaret Vallange, the child, then took a sudden fit of illness which caused her to swoon or faint, and left her in a state of weakness.

Margaret then advised the parents to send for Christiane so that she might cure the child. The mother refused to do so, but Christiane visited anyway, and she made crosses and signs and uttered words over the girl, who was then immediately cured.

Another charge was that Margaret, along with Christiane, was accused of curing Margaret Mure, for which service they had been given a goose and a pint of wine.

In the fourth charge, which was essentially a charge of murder, it was claimed that Alexander Boig had not paid Margaret's husband for an anvil.

Margaret had taken the complaint to Boig's master, Sir George Elphinstone of Blitheswood, but he refused to help. When she was rebuffed, Margaret, rather unwisely as it turned out, threatened Boig in the presence of Sir George and some of his tenants.

Within a few days Boig's child took a mortal illness and died, the cause of which was said to be Margaret's cursing and witchcraft.

Margaret's advocates attempted to defend their client's interests. They argued against, and objected to, each of the charges, some of the witnesses and also to some of the members of the jury. They argued about the relevancy of certain charges and about specific details.

On the first charge they submitted that the prosecution did not specify how the witchcraft was carried out. Witchcraft was done using signs; crosses; poisoned water, oils, and powders; pictures; herbs; words and Satanic invocations but, since the charge made no reference to any of these means, it could not have been witchcraft.

The defence also complained that the term 'laying-on and taking-off' was too general. The prosecution alleged that there was no need to specify the means used because, since witches were well-acquainted with their own craft, they did not need it itemised in detail, so the use of the phrase was sufficient.

The defence also tried to defend Margaret's actions of taking the patient's wrist and laying her hand on their chest. They claimed that these actions were simply the accepted means of ascertaining a patient's condition. Any doctor or friend might take the patient's pulse at the wrist, and check the chest 'which is the stirring of the spirits-vital' and so Margaret's actions were not necessarily injurious.

For some of the charges, the defence also complained that the prosecution relied merely on coincidence – which was not sufficient evidence to prove Margaret's guilt. They also objected to the assertion that because Margaret had asked Christiane Grahame to cure her, this necessarily meant that she was associated with her. Instead, the defence argued that when Margaret took ill, she believed herself bewitched. Since she knew Christiane Grahame had a reputation as a witch, she sent for her in order to request her to remove the enchantment. This only implied that Margaret knew of Christiane's reputation, not that she was a witch herself or knew anything about witchcraft.

On the charge of the murder of Robert Mure, the defence argued that, although Margaret was heard to have cursed Mure, this was not sufficient proof. The prosecution proposed that a promise to do something

indicated intent, and a confession only confirmed the act, therefore a witness to the act
itself was not necessary. It was claimed her
curse also included a reference to the death of
Mure's brother-in-law. Margaret's defence
argued that the man had died of natural
causes – of lung disease – and that there was
no evidence that she had used crosses, signs,
herbs or other means of enchantment. The
defence objections were all over-ruled

The case demonstrated the tensions of
burgh life – the kind of acrimonious
relationships which could build up over years
and the risks associated with bad reputations.

It would appear that Margaret had a sharp
tongue and was not slow to show her anno-
yance. She may not have been very popular
with her neighbours, since they seem to have
been more than willing to blame her for their
misfortune. The defence tried to object to
some members of the jury, either on the
grounds of a known animosity to Margaret's
husband or a conflict of interests because the
jury member was associated with one of the
victims.

It is interesting to note that some of the
evidence from the witnesses was hardly
damning. Hearsay or ratification was used

repeatedly as proof of guilt. Although the defence objected to the competency of the witnesses and the overall lack of corroboration, their testimony was allowed. They were not witnesses to any tangible practice or evidence of witchcraft or sorcery. What most of them had seen, or overheard, was verbal disagreements or arguments, during which the accused swore at or threatened a victim.

Nevertheless, this lack of categorical eye-witness evidence that Margaret was a witch, rather than simply a very argumentative woman, was not to pose a problem for the prosecution.

Charles Pollock, a cooper, confirmed that he had seen an incident between Cuthbert Greg and Margaret, when Margaret had cursed Cuthbert for libelling herself and Christiane Grahame as witches. Pollock reported that Margaret said: 'False land-lubber loun that you are, say thou that Christiane Grahame and I shall be burnt as witches? I vow to God I shall do to you an evil turn'. He denied, however, that he saw Margaret go to visit Cuthbert or that he knew what had happened in the house.

Pollock also confirmed that he had seen John Roberton when he was ill, but knew nothing about how the illness had occurred.

Margaret Dunning, a neighbour of Cuthbert, said that she had seen Margaret visit Cuthbert but that she had not been in the room during her visit so knew nothing of what had passed between them.

On the charge of causing Margaret Vallange's illness, Marion Mitchell confirmed that she had seen Margaret Wallace take ill and that shortly after the Vallange's child had fallen ill in a similar manner. She confirmed that Margaret Wallace had told the parents to get Christian Grahame to help.

Andrew Mure, a surgeon, appeared and confirmed that he had seen Margaret Wallace being given a goose and a pint of ale, but that he knew nothing more about what had happened before.

Robert Dykes, a maltman, attested that he had overheard Margaret say to Allan Spense: 'Away debauched knave'. He also said that shortly after Spense took a sudden illness. Another witness, Thomas Wilkyne, confirmed that Spense had fallen ill suddenly, but he did not know anything about the cause of the disease.

Another witness, John Pinkerton, said that Spense and John Dunning, Margaret's husband, had had a fight because Spense had broken Dunning's yard measure. He claimed that Margaret had broken up the fight and said: 'I shall take amends'. He knew Spense had taken ill, but did not know what the cause had been.

George Thomson's and James Pollok's accounts were that they had overheard Margaret say to Alexander Boig that she would 'do him ane evill turne'. They then confirmed that Boig's child had taken ill shortly afterwards.

None of these witnesses were able to say for certain that Margaret had caused the misfortune or how she had accomplished it. The evidence, however, was sufficient for the jury, which found her guilty on some of the charges by a majority verdict.

On the charges of having laid a disease on Alexander Boig's child and being a common consulter with other convicted witches she was found guilty unanimously.

Margaret was taken to the Castle Hill in Edinburgh where she was strangled and then burnt.

Case 6:
Isobel Gowdie, Auldearn, 1662

The case of Isobel Gowdie illustrates many of the most typical or expected features of early-modern demonological witchcraft practice. Isobel was the wife of John Gilbert, and she lived in Lochloy, in the parish of Auldearn near Nairn.

In 1662 she was accused of having practised witchcraft for many years and gave a full and detailed confession, which included attendance at sabbats, meeting at specific festival times, membership of a coven of thirteen, shape shifting and flying, and demonic pact. She also mentioned several other people who had attended the meetings.

She told the church authorities that she met the Devil in the kirk at Auldearn. Her description that the Devil was a 'meikle, blak, roch man' was typical of early-modern belief, as were his cloven feet. The Devil also sometimes appeared as a dear or a roe. With other witches, including John Taylor and his wife, she raised the corpse of an unbaptised child. They then mixed the dead child with their own nail clippings, grain and kale, which they then used to obtain the corn from local fields.

Apparently it would appear that the crop had not ripened or fertilised, but in reality it was claimed that the grain had been acquired by members of the group. They also used a plough pulled by a team of frogs. As the land was ploughed, the coven prayed that nothing but thistles and briers would grow there.

She also described how they would fly into houses and steal food and drink. Isobel had a little horse. When she said 'Horse and hattock, in the Devill's name' they would fly away as if they were straw. 'We will fly like strawes when we please, wild-straws and corn-straws will be horses to us, if we put then between our feet and say "Horse and hattock in the Devill's name"'. This may be a vague reference to a primitive broomstick.

The witches would steal milk by passing a tether between either the cow's, or the sheep's, legs. Ale was stolen, or spoilt, by taking some of it from other people and gathering it together 'In the devill's name' so that one of their group would get the benefit.

Along with John Taylor, Janet Breadhead, Bessie Wilson and Margaret Wilson, Isobel made a clay figure which was roasted and baked in the fire in the hope that the male children of the Laird of Park would not survive. Later she recited the verse which was spoken when the figure was made.

'In the Devill's name, we pour in this water among this meal, For long dwyning and ill health; We put it into the fire, That it may be burnt both stick and stake (?), It shall be burnt with our will, As any stubble upon a kill.'

Isobel also claimed that she was able to change shape and that she could travel in the form of a kea, or jackdaw, and her associates as cats or hares.

In her second confession, Isobel told the authorities that she and her fellow witches met in covens, usually of thirteen, and that there was a Grand Meeting at the end of each quarter year. She claimed that each of the witches had a spirit which served them, clothed in green, brown, yellow or black; and each witch had their own nickname.

Although the Devil would give the witches the 'best money ever', Isobel reported that within twenty-four hours it would have turned to horse dung.

The witches would use three clippings of corn which they would plait together. They would then say three times 'We cut this corn in our Lord the Devill's name, and we shall have the fruit of it home'. They would carry this ritual out at Lammas time and at Yule or Easter or some other Holy day, and they would divide the fruit of the crops which they acquired amongst them all.

In her confessions, Isobel included several verses or incantations which were used to achieve certain aims. She also described how elf arrows were given to them by the Devil, which they then used to throw at animals or humans in order to injure them. A verse was spoken as the arrows were thrown: 'I shoot yon man in the Devill's name, he shall no win heal hame! And this shall be always true, there shall not be a bit of him alive'.

In order to steal the catch from fishermen the group would say three times 'The fishers are gone to the sea, and they will bring home fish to me. They will bring them home in the boat, but they shall get of them but the smaller sort'. When the fishermen got home their catch will be less than expected as the bulk of the catch would have been stolen by the witches.

Isobel also described how the Devil would have carnal dealings with them. He would often lie with them when he was in the shape of a deer.

She also confessed to killing several men and women, and named the victims of the other witches as well.

In her fourth confession, she named Bessie Wilson, Janet Burnet, Elspeth Nishie, Margaret Brodie, Margaret Wilsone, Bessie Hay, John Taylor, Janet Breadhead, Barbara Ronald, Isobel Nicoll, Jean Martin and John Young, as well as herself, as being members of the same coven. The devils or spirits which served them were called: Robert the Jakes; Sanders the Red Reaver; Thomas the Fearie; Swein the Roaring Lion; Thief of Hell or 'wait upon herself'; MacHectour; Robert the rile, Henry Laing and Rorie. The nicknames they were given included: Pikle nearest the wind; Throw the Corn Yard; Bessie Bald; Maiden or Over the Dyke, and Able and Stout.

Although the records contain many details about Isabel and her confessions they do not give the full story. Isabel's fate was not recorded and so, although it is likely that she was found guilty, we do not know for sure what happened to her. It is very likely, however, she was executed in the usual fashion.

Case 7:

Major Thomas Weir, Edinburgh, 1670

Although there were features in common, not all witch trials or confessions were uniform, nor were all the circumstances surrounding them the same. The case of Major Thomas Weir illustrates the diversity of witch accusations and trials which occurred in Scotland. It was not usual for somebody to confess to witchcraft without interrogation and torture.

Thomas Weir had served in the Covenanting army of the Earl of Montrose. On his retiral in 1649 he joined the Edinburgh City Guard.

Weir was well known for his anti-royalist stance and his extreme Protestantism. He opposed the appointment of bishops in the church, and he joined a fiercely religious group, known as the Bowhead Saints, which was based around the West Bow, near the Grassmarket area of the city.

When he retired, Weir dedicated most of his time to this group. Known as 'Angelical',

Thomas Weir was famed for his preaching ability and extensive knowledge of the scriptures and he would lead many prayer meetings.

Weir lived in Edinburgh with his sister Jean, also recorded as Grizel, and the final tragic events involved both brother and sister.

At the age of seventy-two, Weir suddenly confessed to his gathered brethren that, rather than being a man of God, he had in fact been a servant of the Devil.

This unexpected confession somewhat stunned the assembled group, who would probably have preferred to treat the whole incident as the wanderings of a deluded old man. Although the matter was kept under wraps for some time, news of this startling confession eventually reached the ears of the city authorities.

A medical explanation was sought as a preferred option to a criminal prosecution. If it could be shown that Weir was suffering from delusions, and a mental and emotional disorder, then no further action would be necessary. The medical experts, however, declared that although Weir was physically sound his conscience was certainly disturbed. Weir was then questioned by ministers of the church who reported that whatever it was that was troubling Weir he needed to confess.

Weir and his sister were both arrested and Jean advised the City Guard to take Weir's staff or stick away from him. She claimed that it had been given to Weir by the Devil and was an extremely powerful weapon.

While a prisoner in the city tolbooth, Weir was visited by many Scottish notables, to whom he continued to confess and itemise his sins of the flesh without repentance.

His sister Jean would appear to have been equally demented or deluded, and gave even more elaborate and specific details of their lives. She described their relationship with the Devil, and claimed that they had inherited their knowledge of witchcraft from their mother.

She was anxious to show the investigating ministers the Devil's mark on her forehead, and claimed her brother had one on his back.

She accused her brother of many sexual acts – both with women, including herself, and with animals. Jean also related how she had been visited by the Queen of the Fairies who had given her a magical root which had given Jean the ability to do whatever she wanted. She had placed a cloth on the floor and stood on it and recited: 'All my cross and my troubles go to the door with thee' and after this Jean had become famous for her ability to spin yarn at an amazing speed.

The two were tried in 1670 and local residents began to come forward with details and stories – all of which compounded the suspicions about the Major and his sister.

Major Weir was sentenced to be burnt on 14 April 1670. He refused to repent and so was burnt alive, along with his staff. According to witnesses, the staff turned violently as it burned, and although it was made of wood it took a very long time to be destroyed. The Major's last words were: 'I have lived as a beast and I must die as a beast'.

Jean was sentenced to be hanged in the Grassmarket and her mental agitation continued to the very end, when she began to take off her clothes and rant at the crowd who came to watch the proceedings.

The notoriety of the case did not stop with the death of Thomas and Jean. Events after their execution only added to the mystery of the whole affair.

Soon after Weir's death, strange noises and sights were reported, especially around the area of the West Bow where Weir and his sister had lived.

One of the most frequent sightings was of

a coach drawn by six headless black horses. It was claimed that the coach was driven by the Devil himself and it would stop outside Weir's house. The devil-and-coach motif was not unusual, although it was more often associated with opponents of the Covenanters, rather than Covenanters themselves.

Those who had been the enemies of the Covenant were said to be the Devil's own and, that on their death, the Devil would come to collect them.

Weir was also said to have been seen as a skeletal figure with burning red eyes, often riding a headless horse.

By the end of the century the neighbourhood was notorious for hauntings and other supernatural events, and the house was abandoned. It was uninhabited until 1820 when a family were persuaded to move in. Despite the low rent, the family soon reported disturbances such as objects moving about the rooms. The appearance of a spectral calf in the bedroom quickly persuaded them to quit the house. The derelict building was demolished about 1870.

The Weir case was an unusual one, not least because of the later alleged hauntings and disturbances associated with the area. Witches do not seem to have returned as ghosts after their deaths, but there does seem to be a link between Covenanters and stories about ghosts and the Devil. Those who were the enemies of the Covenanters were often labelled as warlocks and, after their death, many stories circulated which linked them with the Devil. Weir was not an enemy of the Covenanters, but the reports about apparitions were very similar.

Also, unlike most of the other cases of witchcraft, Weir and his sister were not accused of malefice or harm. They confessed to demonic pact on their own volition, without being prompted.

Another unusual feature was that they were both religious zealots. Most other accused witches appear to have been far less extreme in their beliefs. The pact with the Devil was undoubtedly a key feature in all confessions of witchcraft at this time, but the religious beliefs of the Weirs may well have intensified their belief in the power and reality of the Devil.

Their claims may have been due to delusions or dementia, possibly the result of old age, compounded by religious zeal.

On the other hand, they may indeed have had an incestuous relationship, and the strain of the deception and guilt may have eventually cracked their mental stability. Both seemed reluctant or unable to repent, perhaps because they felt they did not deserve forgiveness for their sins.

Case 8:
Witches of Pollok, Pollok, 1676

Sir George Maxwell was involved in some witch trials in Gourock in 1676. Shortly after the trials, he fell ill with an unexpected and unusual illness.

Indeed it was believed that he was bewitched, as he suffered from a 'hot and fiery distemper'.

A local girl, Janet Douglas, who was unable to speak (it was often thought that someone who had a disability, such as deafness, blindness or dumbness, had been compensated with some special extra sense or ability such as prediction), managed to inform the authorities that she knew how Maxwell's illness had been caused. She told them that there were effigies of Maxwell, stuck with pins, at the house of Janet Mathie, another local woman. Janet was the widow of John Stewart, who had been the miller at Pollokmill. It is not known how Douglas managed to communicate these details to others as it does not seem likely that she could write.

The following year, 1677, Janet Mathie, her son John Stewart, daughter Annabel and three other women – Margaret Jackson, Bessie Weir and Marjory Craig – were tried at Paisley. They were accused of demonic pact, renunciation of their baptism and malefice – the harm done to Sir George Maxwell. Janet, her son, and the three other women were burnt, but Annabel was released because she was only fourteen-years old.

Much of the evidence came from Janet Douglas who, miraculously it seems, recovered the power of speech after the accused were executed.

Sir George recovered, but only for a short while as he died quite soon after the trial.

Case 9:
Bargarran Case, Renfrewshire, 1697

O ne of the most notorious witchcraft cases of the late seventeenth century was that of Christian Shaw of Bargarran who, in 1697, accused several people of witchcraft and sorcery.

What may have started out as a case of juvenile anger and petulance escalated into an extremely serious and shocking case of mass accusation and witch hunt. In total twenty-six people were accused; seven of whom were found guilty and burnt in 1697.

T he Bargarran case is also famous both because it was unusual and because, like the North Berwick case, it attracted a lot of attention at the time as well as later.

Apart from the large numbers accused by one person, the features of demonic possession, which it was claimed that Christian experienced, although not unique in seventeenth-century Scotland or elsewhere, were certainly not common place. The involvement of a child – particularly as an accuser – was also unusual.

Following the case, a book entitled '*A True Narrative of the Sufferings and Relief of a Young Girle; Strangely molested by Evil spirits and their instruments in the West: With a preface and postscript containing Reflections on what is most Material or Curious either in the history or trial of the Seven Witches who were Condemn'd to be Execute in the country*' was published in Edinburgh in 1698. The account of the events recorded in this anonymous book helped give the case increased attention and notoriety, especially given the overall decline in the number of witch accusations which were occurring by the end of the seventeenth century.

In 1696, when Christian was about ten, she began to experience strange fits of vomiting and torment which lasted for about a year. She claimed that they started after she had been cursed by Katherine Campbell.

Katherine, who was from the Highlands, was a housemaid in the Shaw household. Christian had seen the maid stealing some milk and the two argued over the incident. Christian claimed that Katherine had cursed her, saying: 'The Devil harle your soul through Hell' and she said that Katherine and another woman, Agnes Naismith, were attacking her and causing her symptoms.

The child was examined by local apothecaries and physicians who could not find any explanation for her condition.

Christian's symptoms increased, and she began to vomit nails, animal hair, bones and straw. She also experienced episodes of spasms when her body would become rigid and her back arched.

She started to accuse certain individuals of tormenting her, and said they were biting and nipping her, and forcing objects into her mouth which she later regurgitated. These included nails, hair, bones, straw, and egg shells. It was also claimed that she was seen to fly around the room.

At times she would either fall into a coma-like state or she would laugh, talk and scream as if she was having conversations with invisible people. She was taken into Glasgow to be examined by Sir Matthew Brisbane, an eminent physician, who came to the conclusion that her condition was natural. He described her as suffering from 'hypochondriac melancholy'.

Christian became the object of speculation and interest, and many inquisitive visitors came to the house to see Christian's strange behaviours for themselves. Local ministers prayed over her, but when verses from the scriptures were read out she would react violently. She said she could see the Devil, and would the apparently have theological debates with it. She began to quote verses from Job and Luke and, as more and more people came to see her, the episodes became increasingly violent.

In January 1697 the privy council ordered a commission of inquiry, composed of many of Bargarran's relatives and peers, to investigate the twenty-one people accused. The other five accused were added later.

The main suspects were Katherine Campbell, Agnes Naismith, Alexander Anderson and his daughters Elizabeth and Jean. Many of the other men, women and children were related to each other in some way, including James and Thomas Lindsay who were cousins of the Andersons; mother and daughter Margaret Lang and Martha Semple; John Stewart and his wife Annabel Reid; sisters Margaret and Janet Roger; and brothers John and James Lindsay.

The others accused were Janet Ker, Angus Forrester, Margaret Fulton, Margaret Shearer, William Miller, John Reid, Margaret Cunningham, Katherine Ferrier, Margaret Ewing, Margaret McKillop and Mary Morrison.

These individuals, including the children, were questioned and over time named the others involved. They gave accounts of sabbats or meetings of the group held at the Bargarran Orchard, as well as details about particular shipwrecks and the death of a minister – many of which Christian herself described.

It was also claimed that while certain individuals were being questioned, Christian's symptoms or complaints appeared to diminish but, when the questioning stopped, her attacks increased again and would continue until the interrogation restarted.

According to Christian, the accused were hurting and tormenting her, but when they were arrested and questioned they were prevented from doing so.

In the end, seven people were executed and another two died before their punishment could be carried out.

Alexander Anderson died in prison of natural causes, and John Reid hanged himself. John Lindsay, James Lindsay, Margaret Fulton, Agnes Naismith, Thomas Lindsay,

Katherine Campbell and Margaret Lang were all executed.

Christian went on to make a full recovery. She married late in life, although was widowed within two years.

Following the death of her husband, she returned to the family home and was involved in founding the Bargarran Thread company. Paisley was later world famous for its sewing thread and textiles, and Christian Shaw's contribution to the wealth of the town was very important.

It is her role in the witch trial, however, that she is better known. The subsequent published account of her experiences only added to the controversy.

The 'Narrative' was taken as an accurate account by later, more sceptical, writers who then proceeded to accuse Christian of being an impostor. They felt Christian must have been, if not evil, certainly hysterical.

In the twentieth century, it was suggested that her symptoms indicated an episode of mental illness.

If the accounts are true then it is clear that in order to carry out such extreme physical manoeuvres Christian must have been an accomplished actress or performer, or she had

104

accomplices. It is this latter proposal which would seem likely, and it may well be that Christian was manipulated by others, in particular the ministers.

The 'Narrative' may have been written or compiled by ministers who were heavily involved in the whole affair. They supervised Christian, sat with her, and prayed over her.

James Hutchison delivered a passionate sermon to the commission of inquiry which stressed that it was God's will that witches be put to death. Hutchison did not pull any punches, and claimed that children were just as likely to be witches as adults, and that it was poor people who mostly used witchcraft. Lust and jealousy were the main reasons why they were attracted to witchcraft. Although Hutchison may not have written the 'Narrative', he was not alone in his sentiments. The church in Scotland had experienced much change during the seventeenth century and many Covenanting ministers, who had been turned out of their posts, were unforgiving of those who had conformed to the Episcopalian form of church.

One possibility is that Christian's anger, resentment or even fear of the supernatural was used for a specific purpose. Either the account of the events at Bargarran was exaggerated or she was prompted to say and act in a particular manner.

Ministers around Christian may have fed her with theological and biblical extracts, or exaggerated her use of scriptural quotations. Christian was an intelligent girl and was relatively well-educated, but her knowledge of the bible does seem extensive for a child of ten or eleven. She was still a relatively young girl and, although her anger against Katherine Campbell and the others may have been real enough, carrying out such a elaborate deception unassisted seems unlikely.

What is more likely is that Christian's experience was turned into a publicity opportunity just at a time when fears about witchcraft and witches were diminishing.

Another ingredient which may have had some influence on the written account of Christian's possession were events in Salem, in New England in the United States.

Many of the specific features of Christian's demonic possession are similar to those associated with Abigail Williams and the others. Abigail was twelve years old when she started having violent fits, which she blamed on witchcraft. Her fits were so violent it appeared as if she was being hurled about the room.

Abigail accused individual people of biting and punching her; both of these features also occurred in Christian's case.

An account of the Salem case was published in 1692 and, like the Bargarran 'Narrative' it stressed the danger to society from the increased scepticism about the reality of witchcraft which had started to develop by this time.

The Bargarran case was not the last episode of witchcraft accusation and trial in Scotland, but by the end of the seventeenth century there was a distinct decrease in the number of trials being held.

Case 10:
Pittenweem Case, Fife, 1705

In 1704 Patrick Morton, a 16-year-old apprentice blacksmith, was asked by Beatrix Laing to make her some nails. He refused to do saying he had no time, but later saw Beatrix throw something in a fire and suspected she had cursed him and put a spell on him.

Shortly afterwards his legs developed a weakness, and he then started having fits. Morton was visited by the local minister, Reverend Patrick Cowper, who may have influenced Morton's subsequent actions. Morton then began to accuse Laing and others of having bewitched him.

Beatrix Laing was arrested, along with Janet Corphat, Isobel Adam, the wife of Nicholas Lawson, and Thomas Brown.

After being pricked and denied sleep for several days, the accused all confessed to the alleged crimes. Janet Laing was released but banished from the parish. Isobel Adam paid a fine and was also released. Thomas Brown was tortured – pricked with pins and deprived of sleep, and died in prison.

Although the evidence against her was slight, Janet Corphat escaped to Leuchars, but was returned to Pittenweem by the minister there. On her return she was attacked by the local community, who decided to carry out their own form of terrible punishment.

They suspended the poor woman from ropes between a boat and the shore, and threw stones at her. They then brought her back on land, although she was almost drowned, and laid a heavy wooden door on top of her, which they weighted down with stones, until she was crushed to death.

Finally, the townspeople asked a man to drive his horse and cart over Janet Corphat's body to make sure she was dead.

Although the episode was shocking in its brutality, it was an extremely unusual example of mob violence.

But who was to blame? Patrick Morton who blamed his illness on witchcraft? Although by the eighteenth century, belief in witchcraft was officially on the decline, it would seem that ordinary people still believed in it or were certainly more cautious about dismissing the potential harm of witchcraft.

Morton's actions, although shocking to us,

were quite understandable and acceptable to many of his contemporaries. So the blame may not lie with him.

If it was not Morton, then was the local community, whose actions got out of hand, to blame? The same concerns about witchcraft which frightened Morton affected the local townsfolk who were driven by anger and fear which, then compounded by hysteria, to mob violence.

What about the local lairds and other men of authority? The minister, Patrick Cowper, witnessed the events but did nothing to intervene or prevent them from happening. Indeed, the crowd may have been encouraged to act the way they did. The local magistrates also failed to intervene. They were educated men, but many educated men continued to believe in the reality of witchcraft. Indeed, no one group or person was probably to blame – although that would be little comfort to poor Corphat.

Not all educated men condoned the action of the Pittenweem community. After the tragic events, a number of leaflets were published drawing public attention to the events, and the following outcry eventually led to legal proceedings against the local magistrates.

Case 11:
Lord Alexander Skene, Skene, 1724

The labelling of a wizard would appear to have been quite different from that of a witch. Although social, religious and political factors were important in some accusations their influence was not always the same. The case of Thomas Weir demonstrated some of the complex religious and political ideology in such cases, but his case was unusual because he confessed to being a wizard without being accused or indeed tortured.

In the other cases, the label wizard appears to have been applied by others rather than used by the accused. Sometimes the label was used because the individual was different or stood out in some way. This belief was often associated with foreign travel and special knowledge – such as alchemy, astrology or languages.

The label was also used retrospectively, usually after death, by religious or political opponents.

Whatever the origin of the wizard label, another common feature of these stories, which do not appear in most cases of witches, is that after their death tales of hauntings and spectral apparitions developed or circulated.

The case of Alexander Skene from Aberdeenshire illustrates the above scenario. Skene was a local laird whose seat was near the Loch of Skene, and is mentioned between 1680 and 1724. Like others of his class and generation, he had travelled in Europe for several years during his young adulthood. It was said that during his travels he had studied the Black Arts – sorcery and witchcraft.

When he returned to Scotland, he had a reputation as a warlock in league with the Devil. It was said that when he went outside into the sun, he did not cast a shadow, and that he was often accompanied by familiars.

Familiars were supernatural beings or spirits, often in animal form, who assisted witches and wizards. Skene's four familiars came in the shape of a crow, a hawk, a magpie, and a jackdaw.

At Hogmanay, the end of the old year, Skene, accompanied by his four birds, would ride in a coach, pulled by four black horses, to the churchyard. There he would remove the bodies of newly buried, but unbaptised babies, which were then given to the birds to eat.

Much of Skene's reputation was embellished after his death, which itself has an elaborate tale.

According to local legend, Skene was visited by the Devil and was able to cross the loch in his coach. This miraculous feat was said to take place each Hogmanay when the coach would be made ready at midnight. Skene would then cast a spell over the loch causing a thin layer of ice to form. The coachman was then instructed to drive the coach at full speed over the loch, but on no account to look behind him.

The coach was driven according to Skene's instructions but, just before reaching the other side, the coachman turned to look at his passengers and saw Skene sitting beside Auld Nick. Immediately the ice cracked and the coach fell into the water, drowning both passengers and the horses.

Since then it has been claimed that the ghostly coach and horses can be seen galloping across the loch at Hogmanay before disappearing into the water.

Lord Soulis was another similar, although much earlier, case. Around the turn of the fourteenth century Hermitage Castle, in the Borders, was held by the De Soulis family. William De Soulis was said to be a warlock and practitioner of the Black Arts. Local people claimed that he stole and killed many of their children after keeping them prisoner in the castle dungeon. Their bodies were then used in demonic rituals.

Eventually the local community revolted and captured Soulis. He was bound in iron and lead, and boiled alive at Nine Stane Rig, a nearby stone circle. A more prosaic version of his death is that he was imprisoned at Dumbarton for supporting the English during the Wars of Independence.

The De Soulis family were certainly forfeited and lost the property and castle.

After his death, there were reports of terrifying screams and shouts, allegedly from Soulis's victims, and Soulis himself is said to haunt Hermitage castle and the surrounding area.

Another interesting feature of the De Soulis tale is that it was also claimed that he studied sorcery under another celebrated Scottish wizard, Michael Scott. Soulis lived in violent times and, like many others, it is quite likely that he was responsible for the deaths and torture of many people. It is recorded that he murdered the Cout of Keilder and his men after inviting them to a feast at Hermitage. It was after this event that the locals may have captured and killed Soulis. The claims that he murdered local children may have been a later addition in order to justify their actions. Similarly, the association between Soulis and Scott, which implied Soulis must have had some knowledge of the Black Arts, would only help vindicate their behaviour.

Michael Scott was a thirteenth-century philosopher. He was appointed astrologer to the Emperor Frederick II, and translated Aristotle from the original Arabic text. Very little is known about him: he may have returned to Scotland and died at Melrose or he may have remained in Europe and died in Italy.

It was his knowledge of the science of astrology which may have given him his reputation as a wizard, and later generations took this idea further. James Hogg and Sir Walter Scott both used him in their writings and in the *Lay of the Last Minstrel*, by Sir Walter Scott, Michael Scott is said to have split the Eildon Hills in three and so changed the route of the River Tweed.

Alexander Lindsay, 4th earl of Crawford, known as Earl Beardie or the Tiger Earl, was another noble who was said to have dabbled with the Devil. Indeed, the ghost of Earl Beardie is said to play cards with the devil at Glamis Castle in Angus, as well as at Lordscairnie Castle in Fife. Alexander Stewart, the Wolf of Badenoch (another dark character from Scotland's past), has a similar story told of him, except it is associated at what is now Ruthven Barracks, near Kingussie.

Like Alexander Skene's ghost, this Lindsay's apparition is said to appear on Hogmanay at Lordscairnie – a significant calendar day which marked the end of one year and the start of another.

These calendar boundaries, or interfaces, were seen as times when the supernatural spirits were at their most powerful. Earl Beardie was not noted as a wizard, but he had a fearsome reputation anyway.

The connection between wizardry and scholarship or learning was common throughout Europe. From the time of the Renaissance to the seventeenth century, both astrology and alchemy occupied the interfaces between science, the occult and religion.

For those who had very little education anything which was not fully understood was suspicious. Coupled with the belief in the ever-powerful Devil then anything which was too mystical was seen to be demonic.

Many scholars were recorded as having made pacts with the Devil, and their learned manuscripts were said to contain spells and charms. Many European countries have stories about individuals who sold their soul in order to obtain the power and knowledge of magic and, on their death, would be carried off to Hell.

The legend of Dr Faustus is based on a German, Georgius Sabellicus, who practised medicine, palmistry, astrology and necromancy (divination using the dead). After his death his reputation was blackened, and it was claimed that he had two animal familiars and that he had dined with the Devil. The stories increased and, in 1587, a printed version of his life appeared on which later versions by Marlowe, Goethe and Man, were all based. It is therefore possible that the stories which developed about Alexander Skene and the others were influenced by this form of narrative.

On the other hand, it is possible that it was the opponents or enemies of a particular person who needed an excuse to blacken a reputation for their own end.

Tam Dalziel of The Binns and John Graham of Claverhouse, Viscount Dundee, were vilified by their Covenanter enemies who elaborated tales of their supernatural powers. Other vehement opponents of the Coven-anters, such as George Mackenzie of Rose-haugh and Robert Greirson of Lagg, have similar stories associated with them.

Tam Dalziel had a fearsome reputation when serving in the Russian army (he is said to have roasted prisoners over open fires), and he defeated Covenanters at the Battle of Rullion Green in 1666. It was claimed that he was in league with the Devil, who protected him at the battle. Musket balls were said to have bounced off Tam without any injury.

Another story is that Tam played cards with the Devil at The Binns, the family pro-perty of the Dalziels. On one occasion, it is said, Tam won the game and the Devil was so incensed that he threw a huge marble table into a pond in the grounds. Years later when the water was lowered the table was found.

John Graham of Claverhouse or 'Bonnie' Dundee was one of those responsible for persecuting Covenanters in Galloway. He was given the nickname 'Bloody Clavers' by the Covenanters, who blamed him for many of the atrocities which were inflicted on them during the religious wars of the seventeenth century.

They claimed that he was a warlock or wizard and, like Tam Dalziel, was protected by the Devil and could only be killed by a silver weapon. In 1689 Graham was mortally wounded, said indeed to be with a silver musket ball, at the Battle of Killiecrankie during the Jacobite Rising.

Index